Penguins!

LITTLE PENGUINS

by Jody S. Rake

PEBBLE
a capstone imprint

Pebble Plus is published by Pebble
1710 Roe Crest Drive, North Mankato, Minnesota 56003
www.mycapstone.com

Library of Congress Cataloging-in-Publication Data
Names: Rake, Jody Sullivan, author.
Title: Little penguins / by Jody S. Rake.
Description: North Mankato, Minnesota : Capstone, an imprint of Pebble,
[2020] | Series: Pebble plus. Penguins! | Audience: Age 5-6. | Audience: K to Grade 3.
Identifiers: LCCN 2019008835 |
    ISBN 9781977109385 (hardcover)
    ISBN 9781977109446 (ebook PDF)
Subjects: LCSH: Little blue penguin--Juvenile literature.
Classification: LCC QL696.S473 R358 2020 | DDC 598.47--dc23
LC record available at https://lccn.loc.gov/2019008835

Editorial Credits

Donald Lemke, editor; Ted Williams, designer; Kelly Garvin, media researcher;
Katy LaVigne, production specialist

Photo Credits

Minden Pictures: D. Parer and E. Parer-Cook, 15, Geoff Moon, 17, Juergen & Christine Sohns, 5, Tui
De Roy, 7, 9, 19, 21; Shutterstock: Agami Photo Agency, 11, Amplion, 4, Bob Hilscher, 13, Designua, 4,
Radek94, cover, ymgerman, 1

Design elements: Shutterstock/Rashad Ashur

Printed and bound in China.
1654

TABLE OF CONTENTS

THE LITTLE BLUE PENGUIN

Little penguins are the smallest of all penguins. They are about as tall as a bowling pin. They weigh only 2.2 to 3.3 pounds (1 to 1.5 kilograms).

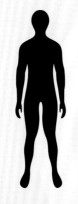

60 inches
(152 centimeters) tall.

15 inches
(38 centimeters) tall.

Little penguins are also called fairy penguins and little blue penguins. Their feathers are dark grayish blue. They have gray eyes and pink feet.

PENGUINS OF THE BEACH

Little penguins live in New Zealand and southern Australia. They live together in colonies. They make their homes among sand, rocks, and bushes.

Little penguins sleep during the day and are busy at night. They are great swimmers. Little penguins hunt for small fish and squid.

A COZY NEST

Mother and father little penguins build nests in holes they find. The holes were made by other animals. Little penguins line their nests with grass, leaves, twigs, and seaweed.

13

A mother little penguin lays two eggs. Both parents take turns keeping the eggs safe and warm. One sits on the eggs while the other hunts for food.

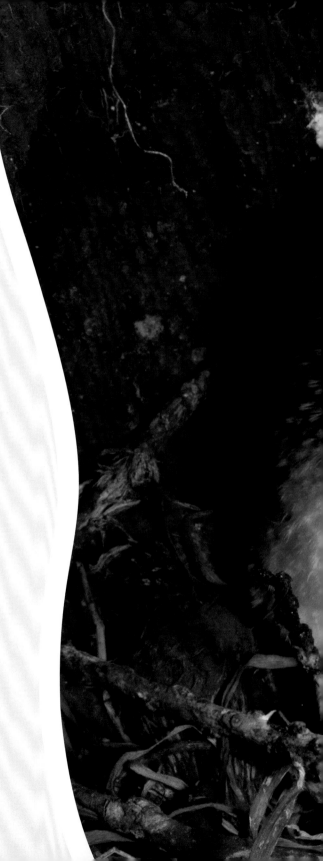

The eggs hatch in about 37 days.

Little penguin chicks are tiny.

They weigh only 1.2 to 1.6 ounces

(34 to 45 grams). Both parents care

for the chicks.

Little penguin chicks are covered with warm, fuzzy down. As they shed their down, they grow waterproof feathers. Then they can take care of themselves.

DANGERS BY SEA AND LAND

Little penguins have many predators. In the sea, sharks and sea lions eat them. On land, dogs, cats, and even Tasmanian devils hunt them. Little penguins can live 6 to 20 years.

GLOSSARY

colony—a large group of animals living together

down—the soft, fluffy feathers of a bird

feather—the covering of a bird

hatch—to break out of an egg

predator—an animal that hunts and eats other animals

seaweed—a large ocean plant

shed—to lose hair or feathers

Tasmanian devil—a small predator of Australia and New Zealand

waterproof—not allowing water to soak through

READ MORE

Idzikowski, Lisa. *How Penguins Grow Up.* Animals Growing Up. New York: Enslow Publishing, 2017.

Riggs, Kate. *Baby Penguins.* Starting Out. Mankato, Minn.: Creative Education, 2019.

Salomon, David. *Penguins!* Step into Reading. New York: Random House, 2017.

INTERNET SITES

Kiddle: Little Penguin Facts
https://kids.kiddle.co/Little_penguin

PenguinWorld
http://www.penguinworld.com/types/little.html

KidZone: Penguins
https://www.kidzone.ws/animals/penguins/

CRITICAL THINKING QUESTIONS

1. What are two other names for little penguins?
2. What do little penguin chick's look like?
3. How do little penguins build their nests?

INDEX